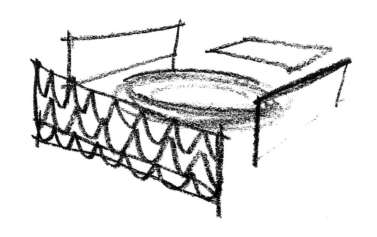

UPDATED AND EXPANDED

PATTERSON

HOUSES OF AOTEAROA

with more than 200 illustrations

For Andres Arcila-Rivera and my fellow directors Andrew Mitchell and Davor Popadich

CONTENTS

HERBERT YPMA

In the mid-1980s, I was young enough and naive enough to start an Antipodean 'design and architecture' magazine, called *Interior Architecture* ... from scratch. I was the publisher, the editor and the sole proprietor ... a fancy way of saying 'chief cook and bottle washer'. Surprisingly, the magazine proved to be a success, and in its fifth year of publication I opted to expand our editorial horizons. Once a year, we (the team had grown to about a dozen people by then) would produce an issue that would go further afield – to look where no one had looked before. I know this sounds obnoxiously '*Star Trekish*', but it explains how and why I first stumbled across the work of Andrew Patterson. In an issue devoted entirely to 'Design in the South Pacific', Andrew – barely out of his twenties – was the 'star' architect.

To me, his work embodied everything that is important about architecture. It is not about pretty shapes or stylish furnishings. Nor is it about slavishly adhering to the latest trend. Inspiring architecture should make you say 'I want to go there ... I want to stand there ... I want to look out at that view ... and I will never tire of doing so!' Timeless, emotive architecture is about understanding the history, the culture and the landscape of a particular place and incorporating all of it into a new end product. Andrew Patterson does this better than anyone, especially on his home turf.

Land is a dominant factor in Polynesian culture. For Māori, land is sacred and the physical landscape commands a respect bordering on worship. Patterson reflects this perspective in his work ... and in his words: 'The landscape of New Zealand envelops us,' he says, 'it invites us to nestle in its folds, to be enveloped in the bosom of her majesty.'

And how! I challenge anyone to gaze at the photos of some of the monumental houses that are featured in this sumptuous volume and not, at the very least, utter the word – Wow!

INTRODUCTION

ANDREW PATTERSON, ARCHITECT

I grew up in the heartland of New Zealand and the first 'architecture' that I remember liking was on the roof of the local meat-processing works during a summer holiday job: huge sculptural chiller units against the blue sky. I'd sketch them during breaks. Already I knew I wanted to be an architect.

Architecture wasn't much in New Zealand and my father was determined I should be a doctor, so he sent me to Dunedin University. Dunedin is in the south of the South Island and as far as you can get from where I wanted to be – at architecture school at the top of the North Island. Entry for medicine was an A average, for architecture a B+. It was difficult, but by careful underachievement I was able to get into architecture.

I arrived back home to apologize to a disappointed Dad, only to find he had bought me a drawing board. Not just any drawing board either, but the Range Rover of drawing boards. It looked like a dentist's chair and I still use it today, much to the curiosity and amusement of anybody under thirty in our studio. Emblazoned on it was Dad's secret to life, Jacob Bronowski's book *The Ascent of Man*, the humanist as scientist.

When I entered architecture school my grandfather was ninety. He had fought at Passchendaele, surviving one of New Zealand's darkest days at war. His hobby was translating Latin. I asked him about the ancient Roman tests for good architecture, as written by the architect Vitruvius: '*firmitas, utilitas, venustas*', typically translated as 'firmness, utility, delight'. He told me that *venustas* was not the word for delight or beauty per se, but rather the word used specifically for the delight of the natural world. Architecture needs to be beautiful in the same way that the natural environment is beautiful.

Geyser is a sustainable, Six Green Star-rated, commercial complex set around two courtyards. It is one of a series of 'Cloud' buildings designed by the practice. Rather than architecture being designed simply as a response to cultural and physical issues, these projects explore ideas in the Maori creation story of Rangi and Papa. For example, the sculptural form of Geyser and even some of its environmental systems (such as the double-skin façade, which uses convection currents for ventilation, heating and cooling) are designed to mimic the dynamic relationship between the earth and the sky.

New Zealand's natural beauty is admired worldwide, but beautiful buildings have been few and far between. What we have in abundance are elements such as the grand natural amphitheatres on the North Island's volcanic plateau, forest plazas encircled by pillars of wood deeply carpeted by ferns, and beautiful underwater rooms corniced in reefs and floored in white sand, with castles of rock punching out of the sea towards the sky.

My grandmother's holiday house was near the burial place of the Tainui canoe (a migratory canoe carrying the forefathers of several of the central North Island *iwi*, or tribes) at Kawhia and I've always considered myself Ngati Pakeha (native-born New Zealander of European descent). She taught me the truth of an old Māori proverb: '*He aha te mea nui o te ao?*' What is the most important thing in the world? '*He tangata, he tangata, he tangata.*' It is people, it is people, it is people.

I want to thank all of our great clients, some of whom have come to us time and time again. You have taught us that good architecture is about longevity. To be truly sustainable a building has to endure, and for it to endure it needs to be attractive to future generations.

When Thames & Hudson approached me wanting to do a book on our work, I was thrilled at the opportunity to share. The only stipulation was that the work be residential. Since we also create many interesting commercial and civic buildings, I have included a few here in order to widen the context in which our houses are viewed.

There was also, naturally, a limit to the number of homes we could include. I've based the selection primarily on what will add up to a cohesive colour palette. I apologize for the ones we had to leave out.

Please enjoy the work. I hope these projects demonstrate our willingness, passion and love as we explore creating environments for people.

The Len Lye Centre is a single-artist gallery in New Zealand's Taranaki province, housing the work of the internationally significant artist Len Lye. Its design is based on ideas of whānau, or people, in relation to its purpose of housing the work of artist Len Lye (1901-1980). Our design for the building is generated from the identity of Len Lye himself. The building is like a person or identity rather than just an object. This is intended to create a sense of belonging and intimacy.

THE OPPORTUNITY OF NEW ZEALAND

'Last, loneliest, loveliest, exquisite, apart'

Rudyard Kipling, 'The Song of the Cities' (1922)

Around halfway between the Equator and the South Pole, all alone in the ocean at the end of the earth, you will find New Zealand.

Unchallenged, the natural world here has evolved more slowly than in other places. Diverse botanic landscapes thrive as they have since prehistoric times, under a sky so clear at night that it is impossible to count the stars.

Māori who first settled these islands called them *Aotearoa*, 'Land of the long white cloud', for that was their first clue that their long journey might be over.

Aotearoa's benign climate is diverse: from a cool sub-Antarctic in the south to a wet and warm subtropical in the north. This diversity has enabled a strange wildlife and flora to exist. Flightless birds, prehistoric lizards and native plants can still be found.

Here we have one of the most beautiful and diverse natural environments there is.

ABOVE Mitre Peak and Sinbad Gully, Milford Sound, c.1905. (Birch, A.E.: Scenic negatives and prints taken by Thomas Pringle. Ref: 1/1-003294-G. Alexander Turnbull Library, Wellington, New Zealand)

Maori believe that humanity is descended from the earth – that people are related to the mountains, lakes, rivers, seas, trees and birds. They belie the earth. Everything that lives on earth is a child of the union of Ranginui and Papatūānuku, the Sky Father and the Earth Mother. We are created in their embrace.

We do not need to draw a distinction between 'man-made' and 'natural'. Everything is one.

We share *whakapapa* (genealogy) with the natural world. We are kin. Not only are we responsible for the earth, we are part of it. And the earth is part of humanity. It is not owned by us, it is something we have borrowed from our children.

This is *kaitiakitanga*: guardianship.

ABOVE Pātaka (Māori storehouse) at Whakarewarewa, photographed 1950s. (Ref: 1/2-116897-F. Alexander Turnbull Library, Wellington, New Zealand)

SEASCAPE RETREAT

BANKS PENINSULA / 2014

Our very first drawings of Seascape consisted of the simplest form of human habitat: a fire in a cave. Completed, it is no more than a porch, a living/sleeping area and a bathroom. The floorplan is the interlocking geometry of both the close view of the cove it is in and the faraway view of the Comb — a rocky outcrop that was originally a double arch, but that was sadly reduced to a single rock spire by the 2010 and 2011 Christchurch earthquakes.

Situated on Banks Pensinsula, on Te Waipounamu (the Māori name for the South Island), Seascape is a tiny beachside cottage. Rather than imposing itself on the surrounding landscape with a designated form or shape, the house is generated by the landscape itself.

The cottage's programme called for a romantic hideaway suitable for any weather and accessible only by farm track or helicopter. A place where couples can be intimate with not only one another but nature as well. Where the roar of the ocean takes the place of the demands of the outside world.

Banks Peninsula was formed by two overlapping Pliocene shield volcanoes, and the cottage itself is constructed from the very same basalt quarried from nearby. Partially set into a rock escarpment, the structure is reinforced to protect occupants from falling debris. After all, an earthquake has already altered the view, and the tiny South Pacific cove is strewn with boulders and buffeted by storms rising up from the Antarctic.

The project incorporated extensive reforestation and revegetation and Seascape is fully self-sufficient. Our hope is that it almost could have been there forever.

PAGES 18, 23-25 AND OPPOSITE We conceived of Seascape as a romantic retreat for couples who want to experience connection with nature. The cottage is totally secluded at the end of a 5-kilometre (3-mile) long farm track on an exposed coast. Through the design we explored the classic castaway experience adapted for the modern world.

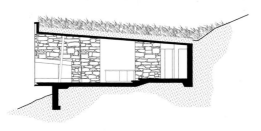

CROSS SECTION

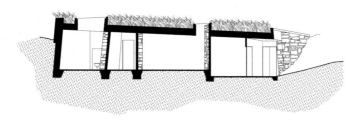

CROSS SECTION

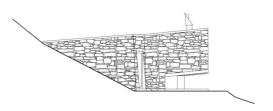

EAST ELEVATION

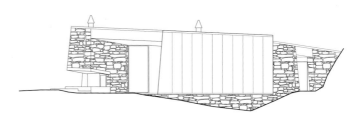

NORTH ELEVATION

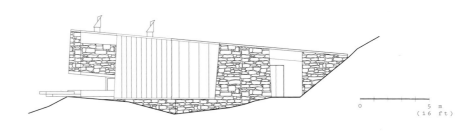

0   5 m
                           (16 ft)

WEST ELEVATION

PLAN

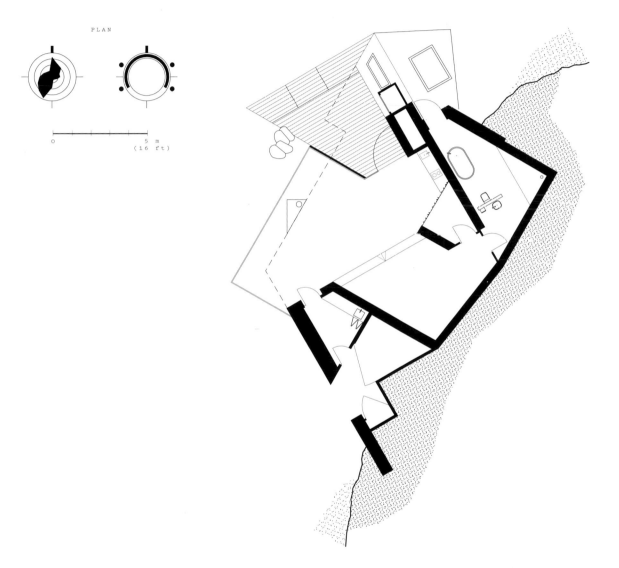

0   5 m
                  (16 ft)

OPPOSITE AND ABOVE The weather arriving from the Antarctic is seen through a triple-glazed, steel-framed viewing wall fitted into a simple cave-like form. **FOLLOWING SPREAD** The cottage's outdoor fireplace and terrace align with the Comb, a well-known rock formation and navigation marker that sits against the sea horizon. The Comb used to have the form of three linked arches but collapsed to a single spire during the 2011 Christchurch earthquake.

The cottage's bedroom space looks over the living room and out to the Comb rock formation. The roof above is thick, poured-in-situ reinforced concrete designed to protect occupants from debris that could fall from the volcanic escarpment above during earthquakes.

ABOVE AND OPPOSITE The cottage is in the castaway tradition – a cave, a fire and a place to sleep. The plan combines the geometry of two views set at 30 degrees to each other: one is of the cove itself, the other of the Comb. This is about connecting people to both views. **FOLLOWING SPREAD** Marine life is abundant here; seals and sea lions, rare Hector's dolphins and bird life can be seen in the cove almost daily and provides great entertainment. The design for the cottage is just another natural pattern on the shoreline.

SCRUBBY BAY

BANKS PENINSULA / 2013

On an expansive sheep and cattle station, nestled in a dramatic natural amphitheatre, you will find Scrubby Bay farmhouse. This is an archetypal double-gable form fully clad with rough-sawn cedar boarding. It blends in with the surrounding sun-bleached hills – not unlike driftwood that has been washed onto the beach by the cold currents of the Southern Ocean.

This is a retreat commissioned by an expatriate New Zealander to create a 'home base' where the many activities the station and the coast offer can be discovered and enjoyed. The only way in is by farm track or helicopter. The secluded retreat accommodates up to a dozen people in two master bedrooms and a bunkroom. Timber storm shutters close the building while it waits loyally between visits.

Entry to the house is through a sheltered leeward porch into the central living area and here guests are confronted by the dramatic view of the horseshoe-shaped bay. At the heart of the building is a central dry stack fireplace constructed from rock quarried on the station, while throughout, macrocarpa timber with traditional rustic detailing lines the walls and is juxtaposed against refined black custom steel fittings.

The furniture is also custom designed: Mah Jong sofas and handmade rugs made from wool farmed on the land warm the home. Outside, a sunny deck extends out from the living room. Here you might find the occupants lounging, enjoying the warmth of the outdoor spa or firepit while taking in the never-ending horizon of the ocean.

PREVIOUS SPREAD The farmhouse is a rugged, utilitarian home where you can wear your gumboots or hiking boots inside and not worry about chipping the walls or marking the floors. It is used as a base for farming activities such as mustering, calving and lambing, as well as for exploring the rich sea life on the surrounding coast. Its approach access can be seen above. **OPPOSITE** The form of the house is made up of two simple gables and inspired by a historic shepherd's cottage situated on the farm. The design for the home is a contemporary model of the original cottage.

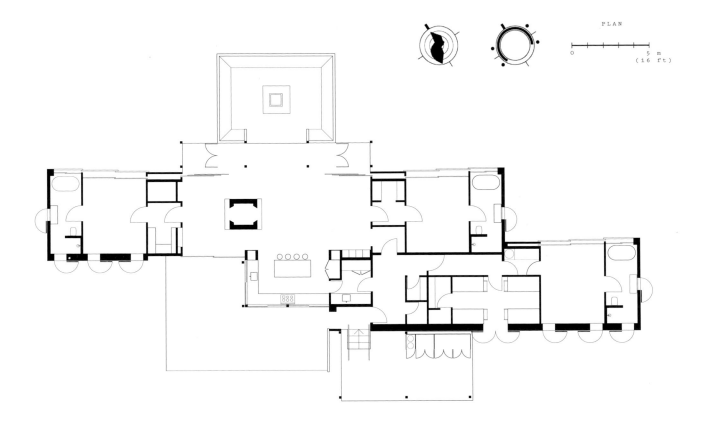

PLAN

0   5 m
(16 ft)

CROSS SECTION

EAST ELEVATION

NORTH ELEVATION

CROSS SECTION

0   5 m
(16 ft)

WEST ELEVATION

ABOVE View of the house and the bay from the hills above. **OPPOSITE** The inland view from the house. The home and its colour, form and concept are patterns of the surrounding landscape and the historic farm that it is part of. **FOLLOWING SPREAD** The steel-trussed windmill is a water tower. It was here before the house and we left it in place.

The three separate bedroom wings can be blacked out with a combination of hinged and sliding storm shutters and closed up during storms or when not in use. The roof and sidings are clad in sustainably harvested western red cedar, which will silver as it ages like the driftwood on the beach.

OPPOSITE AND ABOVE The interior of the home is lined with sustainable macrocarpa timber milled nearby. The main fireplace's stone is hewn from the farm quarry. Fittings and fixtures are all bespoke. The stud height at the ridge beam is over 6 metres (20 feet). **FOLLOWING SPREAD** Scrubby Bay sits as the main actor, centre stage in this natural amphitheatre. It is the spot you would most likely gravitate to if you stumbled upon this deserted bay. It suggests that people (and their homes) can be a natural part of the planet in harmony with everything else.

BETHELLS BEACH

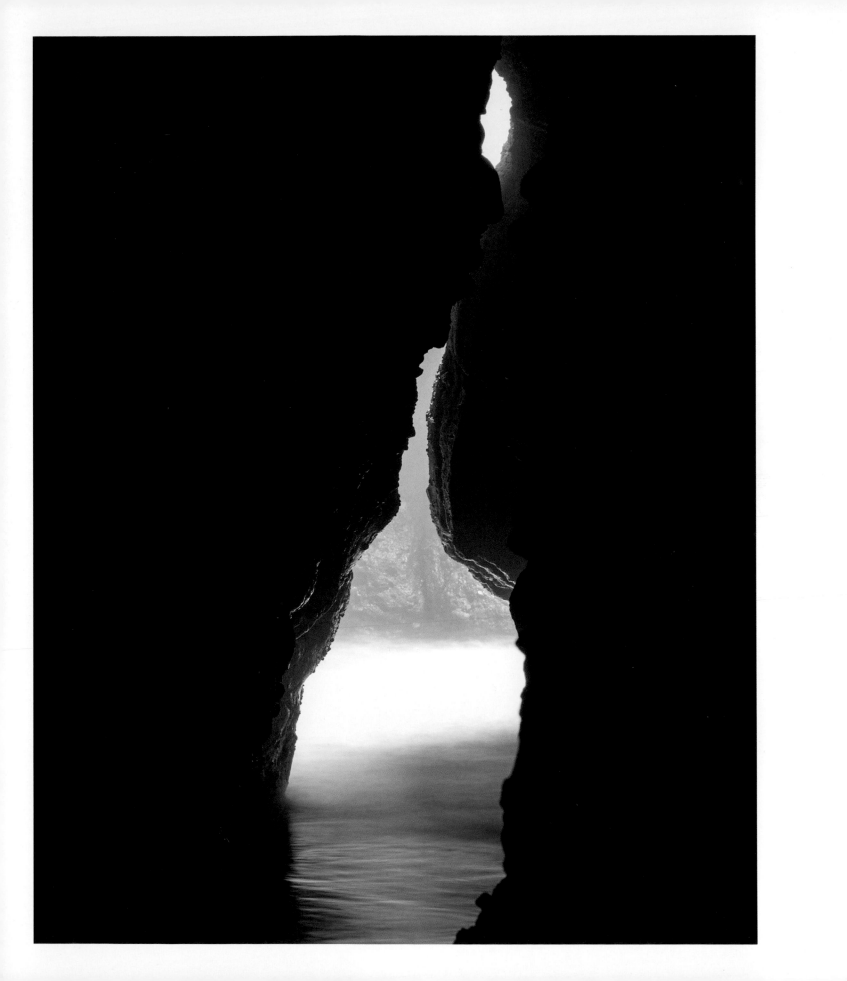

The part of the old volcano on which this project sits is an isthmus separating three wild black-sand beaches.

It is a remote spot, where the surf of the often ferocious Tasman Sea pounds the shore constantly. A system of sea caves, passable only on rare calm days at low tide, provides a link between two of the beaches. When it is not calm, these ancient caves breathe and crash with the ocean swells. During a storm, you hear them howling.

The client is one of the pioneering families of the area and the isthmus itself has passed down through the generations. Eighty years ago, before council rules were imposed, a small cottage was erected on the site. In 1989, during a lightning storm, it burned down. A twist in regulations allowed 365 days to design, obtain consent for and rebuild the structure before the right to occupy would be gone forever.

The brief was simple: exactly the same area and position. The first month we spent thinking. Almost 360 degrees of views were available and begging to be seen, so it really had to be an oval speaking to the old volcano, deferential in tone, more than just a model of the environment: a homage with a concrete, fireproof core hidden inside sacrificial, replaceable storm shutters.

Inside, there is one oval 'great room', two sleeping rooms and a bathroom buried into the ground behind. Each segment of the oval responds to a different beach or forest view. When opened wide the cottage becomes one covered outdoor terrace where the breeze can drift through.

This building throws its occupants into the landscape and then wraps up into a cave when needed. It is a pattern of the landscape it occupies. The family is from Bethells Beach and this is their legacy for generations to come.

PREVIOUS SPREAD AND OPPOSITE A system of sea caves runs under the isthmus on which the house is sited. The house can be shut down with thick timber storm shutters into a warm, cavelike space, echoing the caverns below.

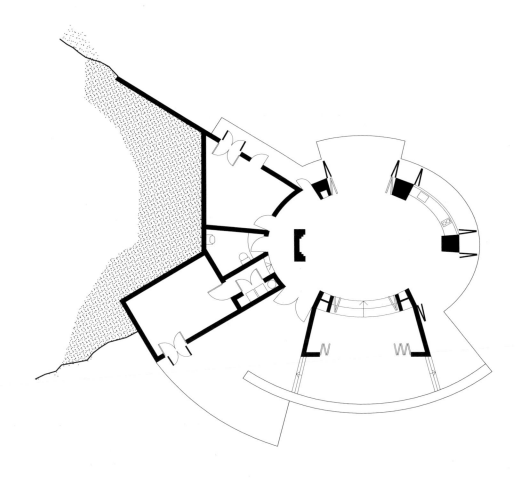

PLAN

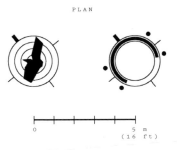

0   5   m
(16 ft)

OPPOSITE The cove below the house runs with surf on most days; it is accessible only via the sea caves, which are passable at low tide.

The environment outside is as important as the interior. The 'great room' forms a simple retreat at the core of the house and folds out to the surrounding environment.

The shutters fold back and open the oval-shaped house up, transforming it into a pavilion on fine days. Each section of the pavilion opens to a different beach view.

ABOVE The home's master bedroom faces a tiny chute-like cove accessible only by a sea cave, which runs with huge surf in storms. **OPPOSITE** A view on the hike to the house that can only be accessed at low tide. **FOLLOWING SPREAD** This home sits on the part of an old volcanic cone that forms the isthmus between three black sand beaches. The beaches are linked by a system of sea caves that eroded deep underneath the cone. It is located on a small plot of private land surrounded by public parkland. All flora and fauna are native.

BELONGING

He kākano ahau i ruia mai i Rangiātea.

I am a seed that was sown in the heavens of Rangiātea.

Architecture, particularly residential architecture, is an extension of our physical presence;
it is what links us to our environment.

When we feel like we belong, we feel
connected, we feel present and we have
clarity. When we do not feel this sense of
belonging, we can experience disconnection,
confusion, even alienation and loneliness.

Underpinning the work of the Patterson
studio is the idea that if our design feels
like it belongs naturally to a place, to
the world, to our time and culture, then it
follows that the people who live there will
feel a sense of belonging and connection too.

At its most elemental level, architecture
is about manipulating a landscape or
cityscape to create environments for people.
Stones are moved to provide a sheltering
hearth, more stones are gathered and you
have a building facing the sun's warmth.
Eventually, you have moved enough around
to create a village, and then a town.

ABOVE Sydney Parkinson (1745-1771): 'A New Zealand warrior in his proper dress, &
completely armed according to their manner.' (Parkinson del. T. Chambers sc. [London,
1773]. Ref: PUBL-0179-15. Alexander Turnbull Library, Wellington, New Zealand)

Judaeo-Christian ideas have dominated Western architecture. The Judaeo-Christian story of creation has humans and the earth on which they exist made separately. The evolution of structures is thought of as man-made rather than as something that comes about naturally.

Over time, our human histories and relationships with the environment have changed, changing also the way we respond to our surroundings, how we assess them and how we design them. In the twenty-first century, as the planet continues to evolve, we find the place we occupy on earth becoming somewhat of a chicken and egg scenario: we might be a product of our environment, but more and more the environment is a product of us.

Innovation. Culture. These are dynamic inputs. Our contemporary environments, especially in urban settings, can threaten ecological and human connections. They force us down different roads.

ABOVE A pattern model of Ranginui and Papatūānuku, the Sky Father and the Earth Mother.

MAI MAI

AUCKLAND / 2007

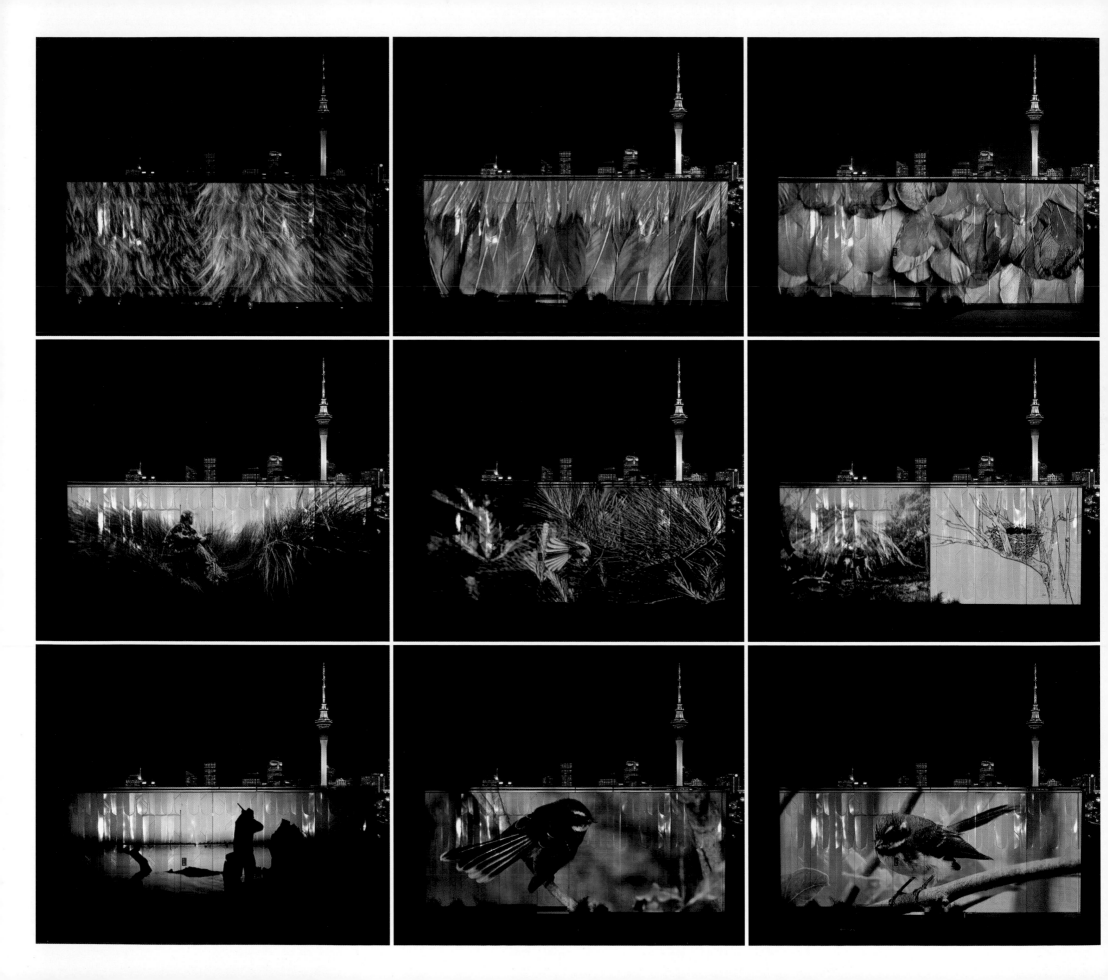

In inner-city Auckland, high on a ridge surveying the city, sits Mai Mai house. It began with a love story. The idea for Mai Mai was to create a private retreat for two distinct personalities — a hunter and a bird — and in so doing, create a singular sense of belonging for both.

A white fibreglass façade is carved with an abstracted feather pattern, inspired by the feather cloak traditionally worn by Māori chiefs. At night, this transforms into a screen as changing images and feather patterns are projected onto it.

Inside, a small footprint, there are many spatial experiences, including wide city views, a nest-like den and a garden courtyard.

Mai Mai is the story of its occupants and their relationship to each other.

PAGE 75 Mai Mai faces the rising sun, which casts its city view into silhouette in the morning; during the evening the same view is bathed in a soft glow. **PREVIOUS SPREAD** Mai Mai's street façade is carved into a pattern of feathers. The electrically operated front door, at nearly 600 millimetres (24 inches) thick, closes invisibly as a secret panel flush within it. **OPPOSITE** The home is situated in the city's restaurant precinct and at night its white carved feather façade is illuminated by projections telling the story of its occupants. New Zealand fauna had no evolutionary native land mammal species — it was the land of birds.

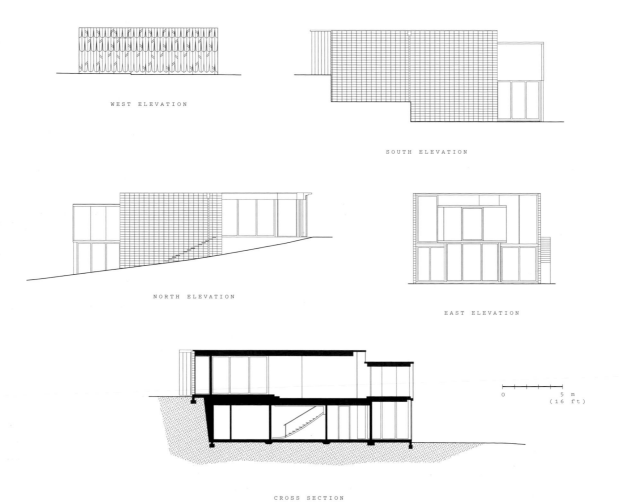

WEST ELEVATION

SOUTH ELEVATION

NORTH ELEVATION

EAST ELEVATION

CROSS SECTION

0   5 m
(16 ft)

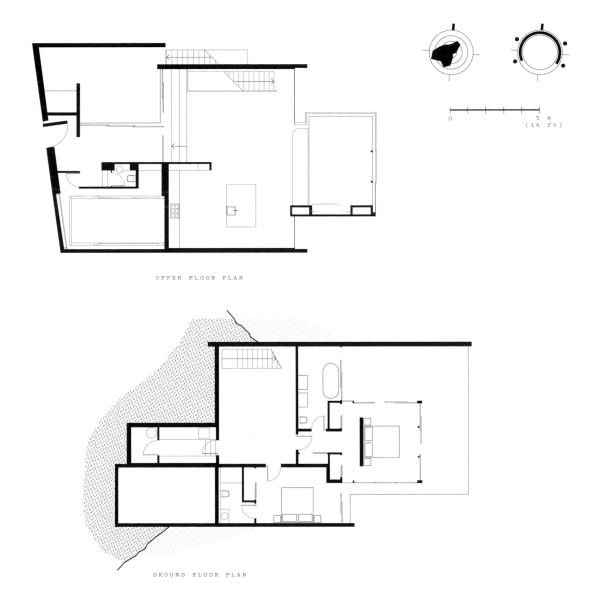

UPPER FLOOR PLAN

GROUND FLOOR PLAN

PREVIOUS SPREAD The third wall of the cantilevered glass cube is a mirrored fireplace. The floor is polished concrete. OPPOSITE AND ABOVE The walls of the upper floor are designed for the owners' collection of contemporary New Zealand art. A glass wall doubles the view as you enter.

OPPOSITE Mai Mai's subterranean 'nest' is a media room where the walls are clad in leather hides. A birdcage-like stair climbs to the viewing floor above. **ABOVE** Mai Mai faces the rising sun.

PREVIOUS SPREAD The sitting room has the feel of a stage set where the actors are in dialogue with the life of the city. ABOVE Feathers of New Zealand native birds are projected onto Mai Mai's street façade, with its secret garage door that opens to a car stacker housing two cars. OPPOSITE Nighttime transforms the glass cube sitting room into an urban space floating in city lights.

LOCAL ROCK HOUSE

WAIHEKE / 2010

Waiheke Island is in New Zealand's Hauraki Gulf, around an hour by ferry from downtown Auckland City. This summer house sits on a steep coastal escarpment on Waiheke's northeastern coast. Access is via a single gravelled beach lane below.

The island is famous for its fine vineyards. Illustrious wines such as Cable Bay, Man o' War and Passage Rock are made possible by a rare geology. Beneath the many vineyards, seams of pyrite rock crisscross the land like veins, giving the grapes (mainly Cabernet Sauvignon, Malbec and Merlot) a distinctive local identity.

A home can bring a whole family together with a sense of place, each individual enjoying his or her own sense of belonging. A home is where memories are collected and stored.

This project is for an expatriate family who wanted a home here not only to re-establish but also to celebrate their New Zealand roots. It is built from the same local pyrite that gives belonging to Waiheke's wines. This is a dense, colourful, hard stone and as it ages it leaches vivid minerals, acquiring a rich texture. Until recently, pyrite was quarried primarily for use on the metal roads that wind their way over the island, but here it is stacked as a series of terraces in the escarpment. Each layer of the house provides views of the beach and off to the horizon.

The home's main living area is tucked safely into the escarpment between a seafront pool terrace and a western grotto-like courtyard that is often used as an outdoor movie theatre by the family. Above this, bedrooms are grouped at different levels: each is a finely scaled romantic louvred lookout in the canopy line of the trees that separate the beach from the hills. Every room is a private retreat in its own right and accessed by an individual stair. The automated bronze louvres control sunlight and provide visual shelter from the sometimes busy beach below.

The home is ecologically efficient. It uses an innovative passive air heating and cooling system by using the rock reservoir as a heat sink to provide even temperatures throughout the year. It has a large rainwater storage facility as well as on-site waste treatment and a reticulated water system.

Our hope is that by using the rock that belongs so clearly in this place the house will offer the occupants the very same sense of belonging here as memories begin to form and fill the home.

PREVIOUS SPREAD Waiheke's roads are gravelled in a local pyrite stone that also forms the gravelled soil type under the island's famous vineyards, giving the wine its distinctive terroir. Local Rock explores the use of the same stone to create a sense of local identity for its owners. **OPPOSITE** The pyrite rock ages wonderfully, increasing in patina with the passing of time. Here it has been used with chocolate-coloured aluminium blackout louvres, which close electronically at the flick of a switch. The home's lee courtyard can be glimpsed at the back.

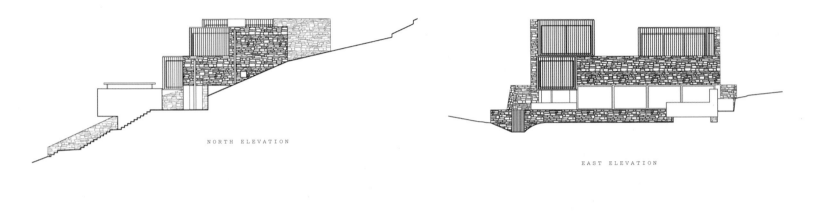

NORTH ELEVATION

EAST ELEVATION

WEST ELEVATION

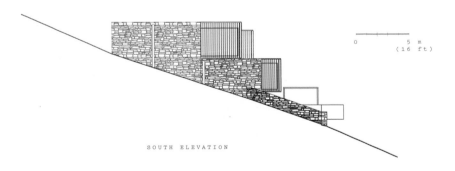

SOUTH ELEVATION

0   5 m
(16 ft)

PREVIOUS SPREAD The home's main living floor sits under a rock bridge open to the beach views, with a protected split-level courtyard behind. Everything you need for a relaxing day is at hand in one simple open plan.

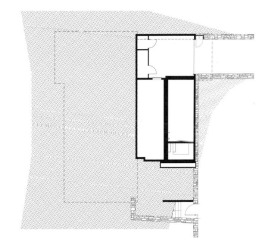

ENTRY LEVEL PLAN

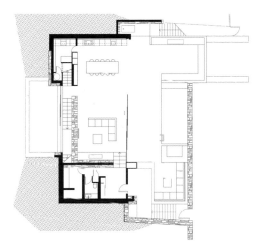

GROUND FLOOR PLAN

0   5 m
    (16 ft)

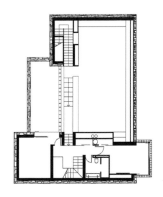

FIRST FLOOR PLAN

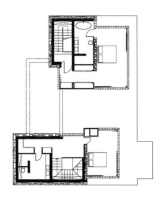

SECOND FLOOR PLAN

ABOVE The home is entered from a beach lane below. **OPPOSITE**
Its gas fireplace is complemented by colour-stabilized timber
veneers and chocolate-coloured aluminium cassette panels.

Each bedroom is located at the top of its own separate staircase and overlooks the beach below through automatic exterior blackout louvres.

PREVIOUS SPREAD Indoor/outdoor living is all on one big indoor/outdoor terrace above the beach. The guest 'cottage' is located on the roof level at left; the owners' suite is on the right. ABOVE AND OPPOSITE A large sculpture occupies the roof space between the owners' suite and the guest cottage. Lazy days in the sun end in still nights and the sound of the waves lapping on the white sand below.

RAVENSCAR HOUSE MUSEUM

CHRISTCHURCH / 2022

Christchurch is New Zealand's second-biggest city. Its European settlement began with the Canterbury Association in 1848, followed by a founding Royal Charter in 1856. An architectural tradition in a wonderful mix of sturdy neo-Gothic and Victorian red-brick buildings developed, houses being laid out with courtyards and gardens around the meandering Avon River. The tradition spoke of substance, permanence and weight, and the city became famous as the 'English Garden City of the South'.

In 2011, after the Christchurch earthquakes, almost 80 per cent of the city's Gothic Revival, Victorian and associated Christchurch-modern-style building stock was demolished in a frenzy. The city centre is now gradually being rebuilt largely in ephemeral, light-weight, seismically conservative construction. A fundamental schism now exists between the new building and the city's previous sense of place.

Our clients' home was 'red-stickered' after the earthquakes - the bureaucratic shorthand identifying it as needing to be demolished. Instead of replacing their home, our clients commissioned this house museum in the city centre and gifted it, along with their collection of art and objects, to the people of Christchurch. The museum is intended as a kind of memorial for the city that was, and as a participant in its re-evaluated story of place.

Ravenscar is designed as a monolithic sculptural form emerging from the depths of the past. It is a place to explore, full of heft, shadow and mystery, inspired by the demolished city and its own remaining neo-Gothic neighbours. It is constructed of base-isolated, precast concrete panels using the rubble from demolished buildings as its aggregate. The repurposing of this material, otherwise destined for landfill, means that its associated memories are symbolically recorded and stored in the building.

To enter, you pass through a deep cleft to emerge in a tranquil courtyard where an impluvium reflects rippling light on a draped mirror ceiling. Although completely new, the building seeks to recall the demolished house through a play on 'ghost rooms': the museum consists of four galleries of the same plan dimension as the original home's principal rooms. These linked spaces, set around the courtyard, are filled with our clients' personal collection of objects. The museum is also a home for local exhibitions and events, stimulating and adding to the city's re-emerging culture.

PREVIOUS SPREAD At the museum's core is a courtyard that is square in plan. This forms a type of impluvium for the collection of rainwater. An awning in mirror-finished stainless steel drapes over a third of the courtyard, reflecting rippled light into the building and blurring inside and outside spaces together. **OPPOSITE** The museum's street frontage is a type of civic house. The building sits on a base-isolated foundation system consisting of eighteen huge rubber ball bearings that enable 400 millimetres (15¾ inches) of earthquake movement in any direction.

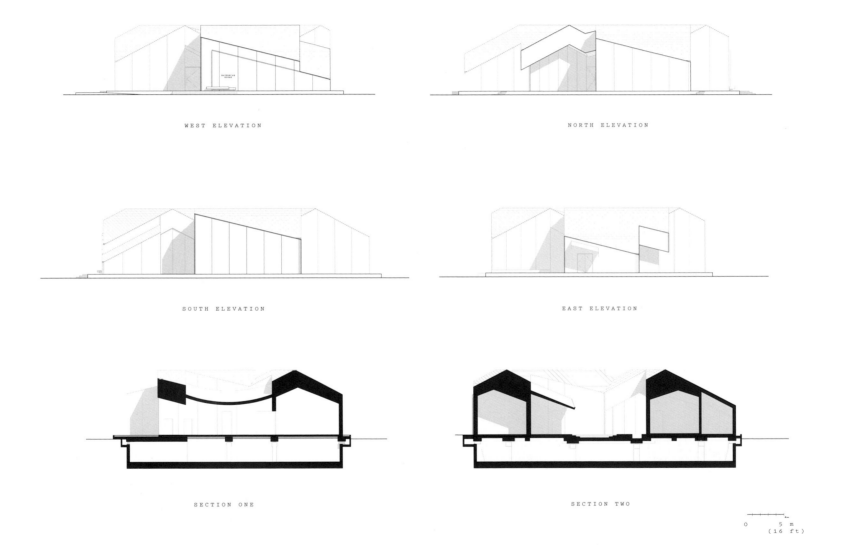

WEST ELEVATION

NORTH ELEVATION

SOUTH ELEVATION

EAST ELEVATION

SECTION ONE

SECTION TWO

0   5   m
(16 ft)

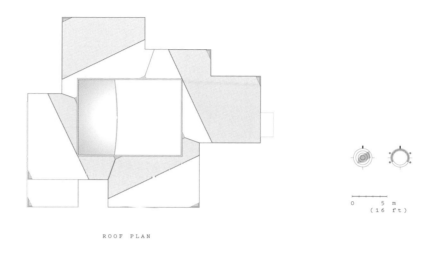

ROOF PLAN

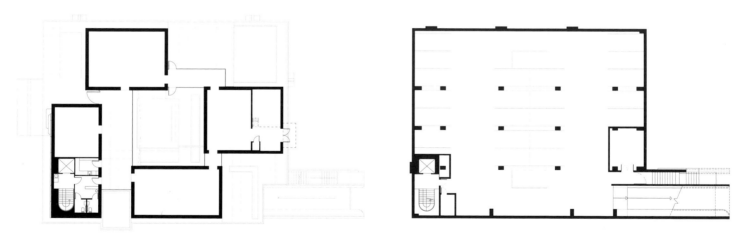

GROUND FLOOR PLAN

BASEMENT PLAN

ABOVE The rotation of the roofs means that each elevation is unique. This northern elevation leads out from the courtyard into the garden. **OPPOSITE** There are four separate but linked gallery pavilions. The roofs of these have been rotated in an earthquake-like twist until the slope of each roof aligns with the next. Visitors enter directly from the street into the courtyard and then circulate through the four galleries.

LEFT AND OPPOSITE Each gallery is a 'ghost room', mirroring the dimensions of a room in the demolished house. Entries to various galleries explore the heft and weight, light and dark, of experiencing the old city. **FOLLOWING SPREAD** Some of Christchurch's last remaining neo-Gothic buildings can be viewed from the museum's lobby. The stud height here is 6 metres (20 feet) at its highest point.

OPPOSITE Rubble from the vanished city was used as the aggregate for precast concrete walls and roofs. It provides visual delight but is also a sombre reminder of what was lost. **ABOVE** One gallery space never changes: a public reading room for the city in the dimensions of the old demolished home's library. Here, people can stop and pause from their busy city lives. **FOLLOWING PAGE** Material from the rubble of the demolished buildings used to build Ravenscar is visible: the black granite of the neo-Gothic buildings, the red brick of the Victorian era and the charcoal grey of the more modern building stock.

THINKING IN PATTERNS

Mā mua ka tika a muri.

The past, present and future are one space we are walking through.

Polynesian language is an oral rather than a written tradition. Pattern and memory play a key part in storytelling and passing knowledge on through the generations.

In Māori architecture the *wharenui*, or meeting house, is a pattern of the people who use the building. Just as elements of the environment such as lakes, rivers and mountains are identities in their own right with human characteristics, so too is the *wharenui*.

The *wharenui* forms the most fundamental private realm and unity of Māori society. Its form and structure resemble a body, arms stretched out ready to embrace; the face and spine of the founding ancestor is at the ridge, while rafters as the ribs are supported by carved panels representing ancestors of the people the building has been designed for.

The people belong to the *wharenui*, the *wharenui* belongs to them. The building is a pattern or model for life and relationships.

ABOVE Malcolm Ross (1862-1930): Runanga house at Ruatoki [Rongokarae whare on Tauarau Marae].

Rather than the Western architectural concept where the focus is on space, light and materials, in the Māori way of thinking, form follows whānau, the extended family for whom the building is intended.

ABOVE Meeting house interior at Muriwai, Gisborne.

NORTHLAND FARMHOUSE

KERIKERI / 2017

This house is for an overseas family. They had a very clear vision for the home, with a detailed brief on both its form and its function. Their days here are about farming, fishing, diving and walking the land with friends and family. They wanted the setting up and shutting down of the house to be fast and effortless.

The 550-square-metre (6,000-square-foot) home is on a 2,000-hectare (5,000-acre) sheep and cattle station that occupies one side of a peninsula in the subtropical far north of Te Ika-a-Māui, New Zealand's North Island. The station is a dry stock (pasture grazing) coastal escarpment sloping directly in to the afternoon sun. A pool house, the pool and the main building are situated to command wide views across the farm and out over the sea to the horizon – a view that would be uninterrupted were it not for the Cavalli Islands floating majestically centre-stage a few kilometres out into the Pacific.

The project is an exploration of ethereal classical traditions of 'a place to contain a consciousness', in this case a family. It is clad simply – a vertically running knotted red cedar exterior lined in local macrocarpa, all hung on twin two-way longitudinal trusses. The truss supports allow the exterior walls of the building to slide away or be closed quickly depending on occupancy or weather. This transforms what seems at first glance to be a utilitarian farm shed into an open, airy pavilion.

The garden is natural and maintenance-free, containing as it does only plants native to the peninsula. The thermal core of the building is constructed from volcanic rock sourced from the immediate area. Local stone also provided material for the basalt bath and 25-metre (82-foot) saltwater infinity pool.

The home's exterior sliding skin is designed to weather. In between visits it blends in like a farm building, while the interior remains eternal – unchanging through the seasons, consistent year after year, visit after visit.

PAGE 127 The setting for the Northland Farmhouse. **PREVIOUS SPREAD** The Northland Farmhouse shuts down when its owners are away, with huge macrocarpa-clad sliding walls. This makes the interior infinitely adjustable and the home's connection to the landscape dynamic. **OPPOSITE** These buildings are designed to look like utility buildings on the farm when unoccupied. A long stone infinity pool runs from the games pavilion out to the view.

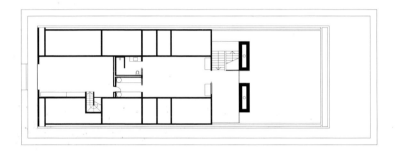

UPPER LEVEL PLAN

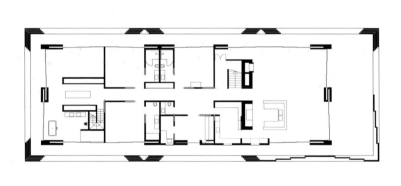

GROUND FLOOR PLAN

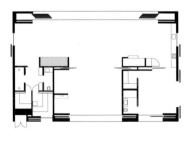

SOUTHWEST ELEVATION

SOUTHEAST ELEVATION

NORTHWEST ELEVATION

NORTHEAST ELEVATION

0   5 m
(16 ft)

CROSS SECTION

The home's interior is constructed and lined in warm
macrocarpa timber supported on large barn trusses with
fittings and fixtures in black. The simplicity of the
detailing disguises the hard work that has gone into it.

OPPOSITE Two matching warm central cores are constructed from stone quarried on the farm. They contain the fireplace, Aga stove and services. **ABOVE** The office upstairs has views to the outside through the building's outer skin.

OPPOSITE The outer walls slide away or close completely. This enables the outdoor furniture to be left in place when unused and the whole building can be secured quickly and opened again just as easily. The view from the games room opens out as the house is opened up. **ABOVE** The basalt pool is a four-sided infinity pool.

The home's sliding outer walls are hung on twin glulam
(glued laminated timber) trusses that run the full length
of the house; all the outer walls slide into just five stacks.
Inside and outside living remains unchanged and protected
from year to year.

KINLOCH

LAKE TAUPO / 2016

Kinloch lodge overlooks Lake Taupo on New Zealand's high volcanic plateau.

The golf course has a rolling highland feel, with rugged surroundings including mountainous tundra. The lodge stands above the golf course, dominating from a windswept rocky escarpment.

It is constructed in bagged stone on blockwork and is punctuated by turret-like chimneys. There is juxtaposition within the structure, which is strong, resilient and pragmatic, but at the same time romantic.

Rather than assembling spaces with an arrangement of floor, walls and roof, the interior of the lodge has been designed as if hollowed out from a single rock form.

Very high portrait windows frame the volcanic plateau in the distance. As if looking through binoculars, the view is brought in very close.

The wind here is bitter and constant. This is where the centre of the North Island rises sharply into a more hostile environment. Gone are the rolling green hills. Facing southward across the deep blue lake to distant snow-capped volcanoes, the building wraps defensively around itself, forming protected, sunny courtyards and battlement-type walks.

PREVIOUS SPREAD Kinloch lodge stands sentinel facing into the prevailing wind on a rocky escarpment looking out to New Zealand's volcanic central plateau. **OPPOSITE** Access to the lodge is through a landscape of volcanic grass, often covered in wild flowers.

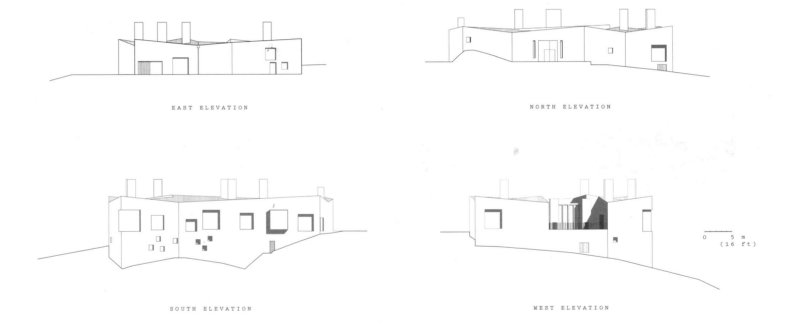

EAST ELEVATION

NORTH ELEVATION

SOUTH ELEVATION

WEST ELEVATION

0   5 m
(16 ft)

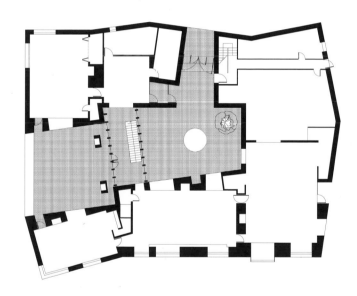

GROUND FLOOR PLAN

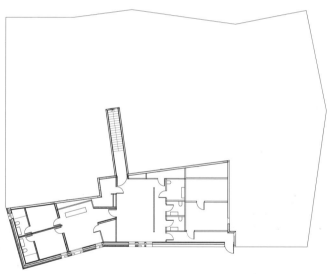

BASEMENT PLAN

A double-sided, glazed cloister that bisects the lodge's central courtyard gives
access to its main reception rooms. Recreation areas and the wine cellar are underneath.

ABOVE Mountain and lake views are brought deep into the lodge through framed apertures acting telescopically. **OPPOSITE** The lodge's great room has two matching and flanking fireplaces, and is walled in plastered stone. Conceptually, we designed the spaces as if hollowing them out from a single masonry block rather than assembling them out of walls and ceilings.

The dining room can be subdivided into private
dining areas by means of curtains.

A central courtyard provides outdoor space sheltered from the prevailing wind and also doubles as the lodge's reception area. In its centre is a water mirror made from a Corten steel disc set flush with the cobbles: when the fire is alight, the flames of the welcoming hearth are reflected in this. The single oak tree will grow and spread to cover one-third of the courtyard.

The lodge's outer walls are patterned in bagged rock
punctuated by viewing windows, some monumental in scale.
All are in the same 1:1.3 proportion. Turret-like
chimneys top the building.

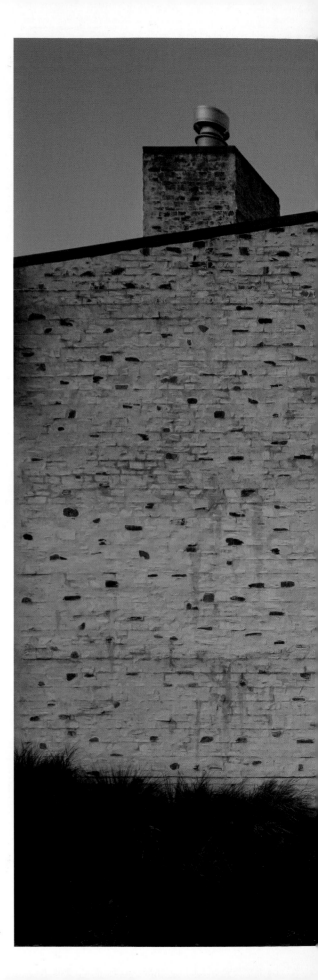

THE MICHAEL HILL CLUBHOUSE

QUEENSTOWN / 2008

Hunkered down into the earth so as not to bother the landscape above, this is a private *wharenui* for a jeweller who is also a golfer. Its design seeks to integrate the identity of its owner into the experience of the landscape and in so doing intensify that identity. It is generated primarily around the game of golf and its own relationship with the terrain.

The clubhouse sits in the Wakatipu Basin, deep in the Southern Alps of New Zealand.

The Remarkables mountain range is clearly visible from the site, and taking this as a cue the building responds to the exciting topography that surrounds it.

Sir Michael wanted a place that could serve as a 'private box' and then convert to a gateway for corporate events. All of the rooms are set around a fireside courtyard, and the external staircase emerges from the ground not only to create but to celebrate a gateway to the temporary tent village that is erected on the grounds during tournaments.

The building's plan is anthropomorphic around a central service spine: carts are located at the foot of the building, the restaurant at the head and spa rooms in the centre. In plan, section and elevation this design adheres to the geometry of interrelated skewed quadrilaterals. It is a pattern of Papatūānuku, the Earth Mother.

Large expanses of frameless glass invite the mountains outside to come in.

We wanted the form to appear to have evolved from the same forces that generated the land around it both geologically and metaphorically. The Earth Mother is represented by sensual curves and materials, while the splintering angles reflect the ongoing geological uplift that continues to form the mountains around it as they seek to push the sky away.

PREVIOUS SPREAD This clubhouse explores the New Zealand creation story of Rangi and Papa: the Earth Mother and the Sky Father prised apart by tectonic forces as a sculptural composition. Earthquakes are common in this part of New Zealand's Southern Alps and the building sits near a fault line known as 'the Great Divide'. **OPPOSITE** Two elevations of the clubhouse hunker down into the earth allowing the game of golf to be played around it (or on it!).

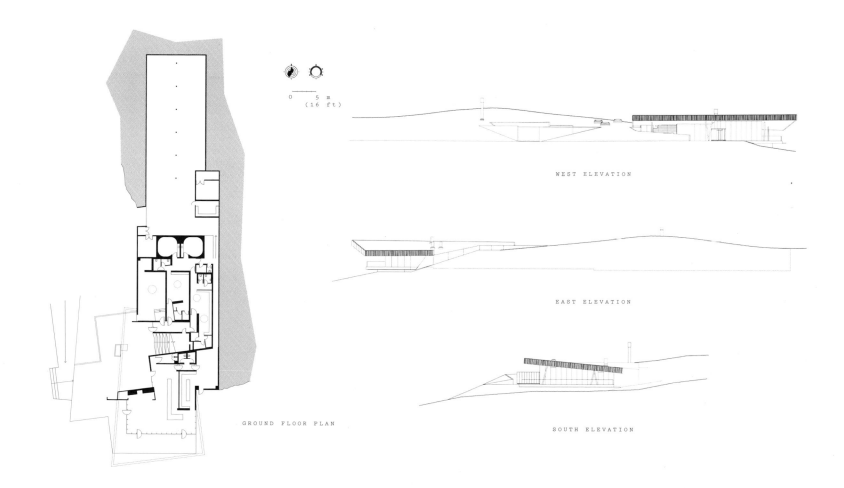

0   5 m
(16 ft)

WEST ELEVATION

EAST ELEVATION

GROUND FLOOR PLAN

SOUTH ELEVATION

OPPOSITE This project is a 'private box' for an avid golfer who is also a jeweller. Here the view looking to the 18th green is shown. **FOLLOWING SPREAD** It is not unusual for members here to play golf off the roof during post-game drinks and dinner.

NAISOSO

FIJI / 2017

Our clients Raina and Tejash were living in Fiji with Tejash's parents and, although a very close family, they wanted a home of their own.

Both of their families had lived for generations in Fiji, but, like many, they had been educated and developed their successful careers overseas. They chose to come back to their homeland while maintaining an international outlook and sensibility. Fiji is perfectly located for such an ideal, centrally placed for the USA, Asia, Australia and New Zealand.

They came to us with a slice of an extraordinary tropical island paradise, the stuff of dreams — a rectangular, level plot of 3,000 square metres (32,000 square feet), facing the setting sun. On one side, you step directly onto a private crescent-shaped beach where the sand is as white as sugar and the view reaches across to the Mamanuca and Yasawa Island groups. On the other, land side, you look east over a tidal river winding towards a tropical mountain range known as the Sleeping Giant. Of particular delight for Tejash is the site's proximity to the airport.

Raina and Tejash wanted a large, secure home for children and for a very large family who could come to stay for long periods. They wanted their home to be 'Fijian', and also to be contemporary and of its age, to contribute to the increasingly hopeful Fiji that they represent internationally.

The concept of a clean white space opening to both sides was arrived at quite quickly, but the design kept growing as we started to realize just how many people this couple could gather around them. We devised a house with a simple in-situ poured-concrete structural frame and envelope. Onto this we bolted pre-made aluminium windows to grade 8 cyclone standard. These sit beneath aluminium security fins bolted in place to act as storm shutters and sun shades. A simple coral stone wall adds texture to an all-white interior on cool concrete floors set around the enormous L-shaped horizon pool. Deep in the house, in protected spaces, are all the electronics and services.

Building in Fiji comes with its challenges, not the least of them being 'Island time' — construction does not happen quickly and is subject to a handful of local peculiarities. Tolerances and materials have to be kept basic, construction has to be kept basic. Then there are the island's regular cyclones, tropical downpours and floods to deal with.

The construction process was testing. But with huge credit to the builder and the owners, we managed to stay true to the original vision.

PREVIOUS SPREAD This house consists of a beach pavilion and recreation room to the left with guest cottage on the right. The main reception rooms are in the middle and the owners' suite is upstairs. **OPPOSITE** The view from the main entry to the Mamanuca and Yasawa Islands over a raised infinity pool. The pool combines with the beach pavilion to form a T shape.

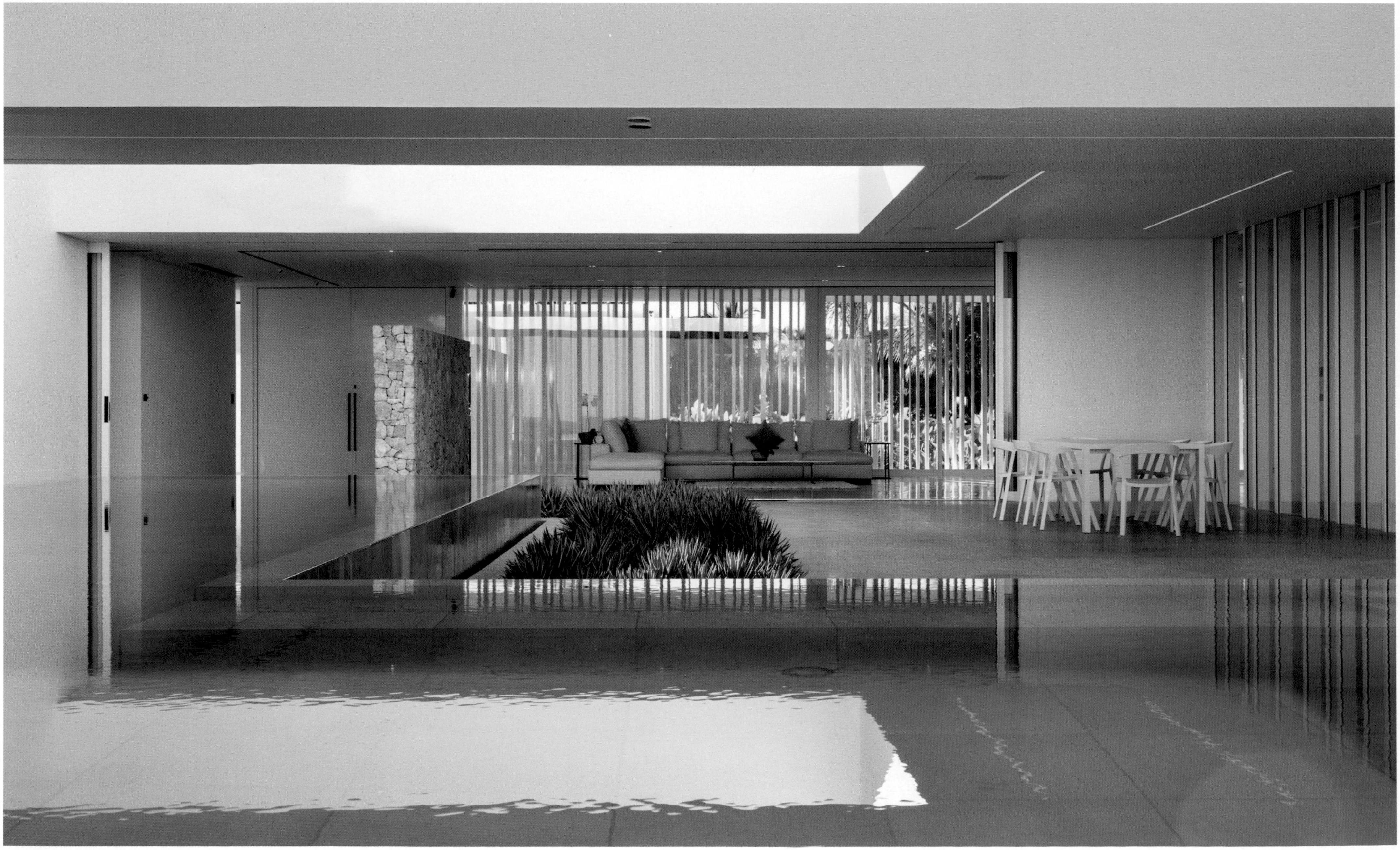

All exterior doors slide into recess pockets, completely transforming
the interior to exterior, free of glass for most of the year. The beach-
front pavilion includes a recreation room and an outdoor kitchen.

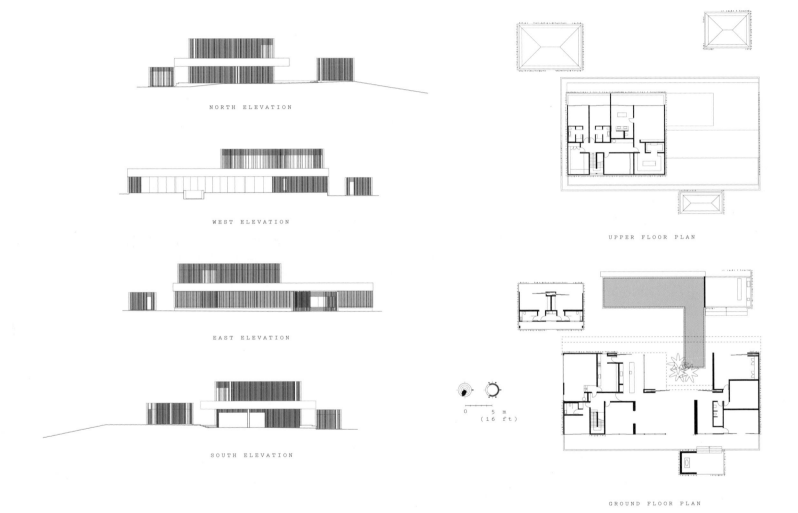

NORTH ELEVATION

WEST ELEVATION

EAST ELEVATION

SOUTH ELEVATION

UPPER FLOOR PLAN

GROUND FLOOR PLAN

0   5 m
(16 ft)

OPPOSITE AND FOLLOWING SPREAD The house looks towards the sunset over a soft-white-sand beach. It uses aluminium cyclone shutters as its aesthetic; these are set on a simple poured-concrete shell painted white. The effect is almost curtain-like.

THE SEARCH FOR BEAUTY

'The object we love is uniquely beautiful,
but that beauty is not unique to the object,
rather, it is a universal beauty'

Plato, *Symposium* (c.385-370 BCE)

One of the traditional goals of building is to create beauty. The emphasis on what
is beautiful has shifted through the ages between proportion, moral and physical
truths and the eye of the beholder.

What does this mean in today's world? What is beauty? Is it even important? Is being
beautiful really a definitive test for good design?

New Zealand is one of a handful of countries on earth with beauty as a defining
characteristic. Allow anyone just one adjective to describe New Zealand and they will
almost certainly choose 'beautiful'. For us, our country provides an opportunity to
understand what beauty actually is.

The Darwinian view of beauty suggests that it is an evolved survival mechanism.
You know something is beautiful unconsciously in much the same way that the flight
or fight response is unconscious. It is an instinct.

Nobel Prize-winning physicist Murray Gell-Mann observes that in the field of quantum
physics, where empirical testing of particles is not possible, beauty is commonly the
criterion for a successful theory: 'What is especially striking and remarkable is that
in fundamental physics a beautiful or elegant theory is more likely to be right than
a theory that is inelegant.' He describes the attributes of beauty as these: universal
(for example, gravity applies as much to the moon as to Newton's apple); being the
simplest expression possible; and having clarity and symmetry.

Our brain looks for simple patterns to recognize, and when it does, it is the
familiarity or symmetry, or lack of it, that quickly tells us whether to admire
or fear whatever it is that we are looking at.

Many ancient spiritual practices have held that the higher your level of
consciousness, the greater level of beauty you can perceive. Today, this can be
manipulated with mindfulness. Neurologists call this an upward spiral. It applies
to beauty, together with other positive emotions, such as gratitude, trust, hope,
truth and, of course, love.

When we look at it this way, beauty in architecture is like our environment giving
us a warm hug.

If universal beauty is a sense of consciousness, maybe collective recognition of
such beauty confirms the Darwinian hard-wired theory. Just as the proportions of the
human body can elicit a sensual feeling, other qualities of human consciousness,
such as honesty, truth, generosity and love, are recognized collectively as pattern
models in our brain and generate a feeling of belonging. And when we belong, we easily
recognize beauty. Recent phenomenology, the study of the structure of consciousness
and experience, suggests that a building's beauty relates directly to the relationship
it has with its physical and human environments — a relationship that starts with
the architect and eventually connects him or her with the people for whom the
building was intended.

THE PINES

MATARANGI / 2005

The coastline of New Zealand is a crown studded with jewels and everyone has their personal favourite.

All around the coast are communities of the summer houses known locally as baches. Some of these have simply sprouted from campsites and become groups of tiny ramshackle cottages huddled together. Baches can stay in families for generations. They are often erected quickly and intended only as temporary structures but then added to over the years. They are character-rich and crammed with memorabilia.

The bach is a tool for keeping families together, as succeeding generations spend their summer days fishing, cooking and playing cricket or touch rugby on the beach. These buildings are base camps from which the environment can be explored and enjoyed. In common they have the need to provide shelter in onshore and offshore winds, the need to be as maintenance-free as possible, and the need to be able to draw all sorts of different family life stages together at once. Children and teenagers can roam freely, never far from the sight of neighbouring friends, while adults can mix without the need to drive, all in a relaxed Arcadian environment where the door of every house is always open.

This particular bach is located on land previously used as a pine plantation fronting a white-sand surf beach called Matarangi. The remaining pines give a violet dappled light.

It consists of a main house, a sleep-out that acts as an outdoor entry lobby, and a boatshed with a two-bedroomed guest cottage above. The main house can be completely opened up along the front to a common reserve over a sociable, inviting deck. Its form is organized into two corrugated-zinc-clad volumes connected by a living space. The zinc cladding carries through to the interior, giving the effect that perhaps these were two separate, romantic structures joined later to become one.

Communal space continues to the protected courtyard area at the back with its external stone fireplace. This is the lee side of the building, through which the other buildings are accessed. Everything is positioned to afford glimpses of the ocean; every room has a different quality and relationship with the rest of the building. There is no front door.

The zinc ages gracefully so never needs to be painted. Inside, the walls are lined in painted larch and covered in local artwork, while furniture cast-offs litter the floor. Shutters on hydraulic stays close down windows, offering protection from the salt spray blown in from the beach out front. There are no downpipes, for they would only be blocked by pine needles. The bach remains constant from one summer to the next, waiting out the cooler months knowing that soon it will occupy its place at the centre of the family again.

PAGE 179 AND PREVIOUS SPREAD This house is constructed from solid corrugated gunmetal zinc. It was built in the early 1990s in an old *Pinus radiata* forestry plantation. **OPPOSITE** Every morning the home awakens to the sound of birdsong over rumbling surf. Each pavilion that makes up the house is a different room; some are connected to create larger spaces.

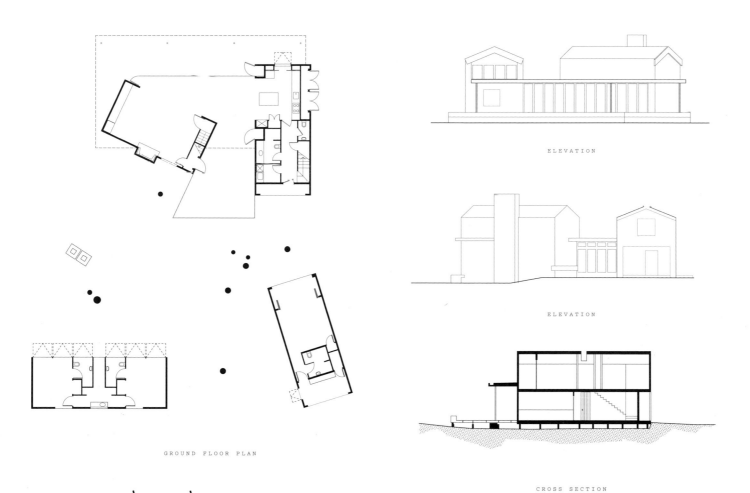

ELEVATION

ELEVATION

CROSS SECTION

GROUND FLOOR PLAN

0   5 m
        (16 ft)

OPPOSITE A long verandah runs parallel to the beach, and doors can be slid back into the walls during the summer months. In the evening the surrounding old forestry plantation is dappled in a violet and gold glow.

The home's outdoor living is created by the spaces between the buildings. There are four buildings in total: a living room with the master suite above; the kitchen and the children's bedrooms; a sleep-out backed by the property's outdoor entry lobby; and a two-bedroomed guest pavilion over the boatshed. There are no gutters on the roof so that the building can easily shed pine needles.

PREVIOUS SPREAD The old pine plantation fronts a white-sand surf beach just below the view. Balustrades form long daybeds. ABOVE A view of the property's wonderful white-sand surf beach. OPPOSITE The living building links through to the kitchen via an indoor/outdoor verandah that forms the main living space. The house is filled with Pacific memorabilia collected by the family.

ST STEPHEN'S

AUCKLAND / 2014

Sonja and Glenn are wonderful supporters of our work. This is their family home and sits in a stately street lined with plane trees.

Living happily just a few doors up the street in the house where they had raised their four children, when this property came on to the market they saw it as an opportunity to refine their ideas on how they wanted to live. Here, they can provide for the frequent return visits of their now university-aged children, often with friends in tow. With family, gardening and cooking central to their lives, the possibility of a bigger outdoor area also greatly appealed.

While Sonja and Glenn held strong views on how they wanted to live in their home, they were very open to the creative process. Their only two non-negotiables: that the home be full of light and sun, and that it be strongly connected to the land. With this in mind we set about creating a pavilion in a garden – a country house in an urban setting.

The design is inspired by the symmetry of late-1960s Italian modernist buildings. For the exterior, we created a pattern from alternating windows and glass-reinforced concrete panels within a steel-framed structure. The front of the house is open and informal in comparison to the high fences and security gates of neighbouring properties – this suits the owners' open way of life.

A formal motor court is flanked on either side by green-roof garages, and the street-facing walls of the garages continue to soften as their ficus cover spreads, a clue to the thriving gardens found behind them. The gently sloping site gave us the opportunity to step the living areas down below entrance level, allowing the home's volume to open up to an unexpected 3.8-metre (12½-foot) high ceiling.

Early on in the process we had discussed the indefinable qualities of new and old in existing homes and the interesting juxtapositions that are often lacking in contemporary home design. This discussion translated into the challenge of creating a brand new home that possesses a personality that is timeless, light-filled and classic, but with an obvious soul.

PREVIOUS SPREAD The home is symmetrical on all four sides and sits on a leafy plane-tree-lined avenue. The motor court sits slightly below the level of the road. The ficus will grow to cover the garages and gym flanking the motor court. **OPPOSITE** The structure of St Stephen's is formed from a steel scaffold painted in micaceous iron oxide and hung with panels of concrete that form a geometric pattern of alternating balconies. The window joinery is steel as well.

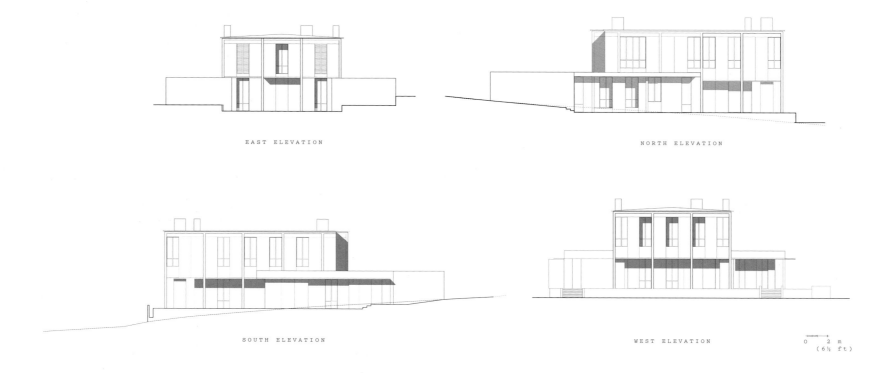

EAST ELEVATION

NORTH ELEVATION

SOUTH ELEVATION

WEST ELEVATION

0   2 m
(6½ ft)

UPPER LEVEL PLAN

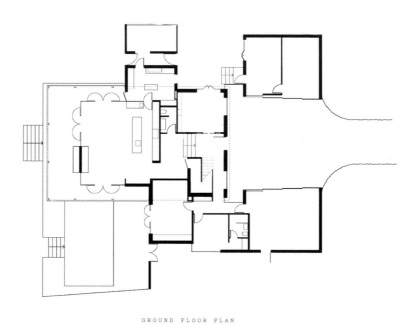

GROUND FLOOR PLAN

0   5 m
      (16 ft)

The main living room has a 3.8-metre (12½-foot) high ceiling and has a blackened steel fireplace as its focal point. The 'nursery plant' to the right of the fireplace is a bronze artwork by Michael Parekowhai.

An eclectic kitchen, developed in collaboration with Sonja, an interior designer, is the centre of family life. The butler's pantry, separated by the glass wall on the left, is part of the garden's circulation and doubles as a gardening workroom.

ABOVE AND OPPOSITE St Stephen's sits in the middle of a rectangular garden planted mainly in flowers and edibles. Conceptually it is a 'farmhouse in the city'. Life here is about family, friends and food. The exterior is symmetrical on all four elevations.

WAIHEKE

WAIHEKE / 2017

This project is intended to be approached mainly by air — by helicopter, or even perhaps, one day, autonomous electric jet.

It is located on Waiheke Island and created for a family of adults who wish to participate in city life, but from a distance. This family wish to live together, but independently, with two houses operating as one.

It sits on a 4-hectare (10-acre) waterfront site facing west and is designed in response to an enormous 240-degree sea and island view. Acknowledging this, the plan is arranged around a trio of outdoor spaces, with two courtyards and a coastal terrace where shelter and view combinations can be found in any wind.

The building's simple form is a cedar-clad, monolithic timber slab or box hovering above the living and entertaining areas below. Inside it is the home's entry lobby from the landing pad above.

Services are contained in the wooden slab, and a series of large, deeply recessed rectangular skylights provide light, without direct sun, to the spaces below. The box works with the home's subterranean service areas, which are located beneath the helicopter pad.

PREVIOUS SPREAD This island home is designed to be accessed mainly by helicopter: the landing pad leads to the home's front door. The roof of the house is its principal façade and is expressed in a wood-grain pattern. **OPPOSITE** The home's bulk is divided into two parts: one underground and the other sheltering below a thick roof designed to modulate the strong New Zealand sunlight penetrating into the interior.

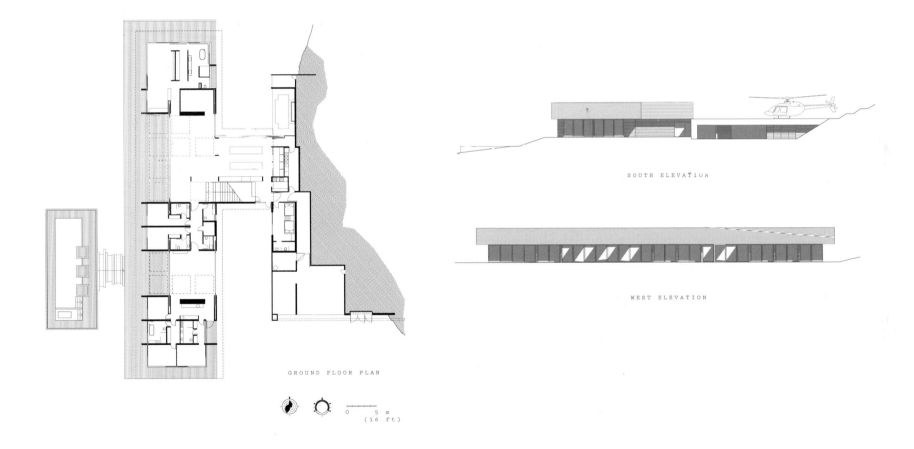

GROUND FLOOR PLAN

0   5 m
(16 ft)

SOUTH ELEVATION

WEST ELEVATION

OPPOSITE At night the main entry stair down from the helicopter pad is lit with 870 flickering LED lights, just discernible in this daylight shot.

ABOVE, OPPOSITE AND FOLLOWING SPREAD The home enjoys a panoramic view of New Zealand's inner Hauraki Gulf and islands. The horizontality of the view informs the horizontality of the house. In its double-sided main living room, glass walls slide back into hidden pockets. The same timber boarding used to clad the house inside and out was also used for the shuttering and moulds for the concrete work. This makes all the exteriors and interiors one seamless pattern.

This outdoor room is the perfect place to listen to music with a glass of wine conveniently located on a shelf behind you. The thickness of the home's roof allows the interior volume to open up to unexpected heights, including to the helicopter pad above.

The plan of the house is actually two connected homes, one for
parents and one for children, with two shared guest bedrooms
accessing both. The children's end enjoys the swimming pool.

PARIHOA

MURIWAI / 2009

Located on Auckland's rugged and stormy western coast, this home is the owners' facility for a large sheep and cattle station. The project explores the architectural typology of a fort or outpost, a form that is at once commanding and defensive.

Sixty metres (200 feet) below, wind and ocean crash to shore from the Tasman Sea. The shape of the building wraps around itself to offer protection from an unforgiving, exposed environment. There is no modification to the landscape, other than the sentry form of the building itself.

Simple strategies of converging and expanding walls create various spatial experiences. The entry lobby is guarded by a gate, keeping the sheep out, and sectioned perimeter walls pivot open to offer an unexpected link.

Long views reach uninterrupted to the sunset. Towards the edges of the structure, ocean, sky and hills open above, below, all around, until the immense grandeur of the environment is fully revealed simply as part of the experience of day-to-day living.

PREVIOUS SPREAD This farmhouse is for a 5,000-hectare (12,350-acre) sheep and cattle farm located on New Zealand's exposed West Coast. There is no garden; instead the house floor is raised and animals can roam freely around its perimeter. **OPPOSITE** The site is exposed to incredible still, clear days and beautiful sunsets as well as to howling Tasman Sea storms.

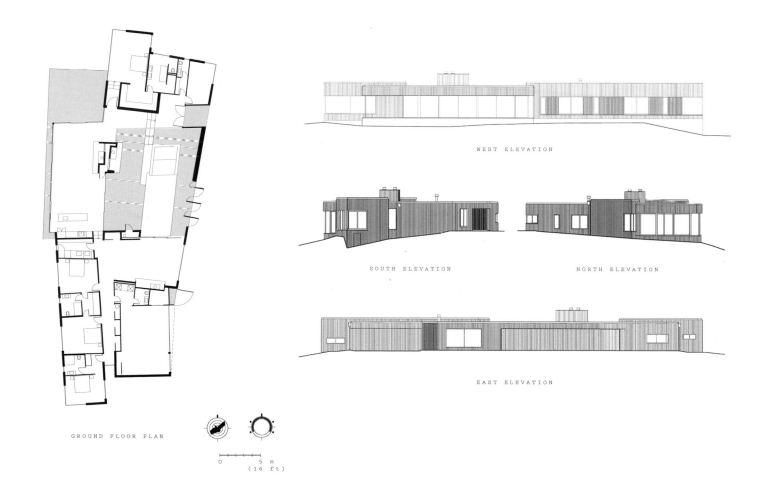

WEST ELEVATION

SOUTH ELEVATION   NORTH ELEVATION

EAST ELEVATION

GROUND FLOOR PLAN

0   5 m
   (16 ft)

OPPOSITE The home's plan is laid out in wings around a sheltered courtyard containing a pool. Each wing offsets slightly to face a different aspect of the views. This makes each section feel separate from the others. The home is filled with secret doors opening both internally and externally.

The view can be enjoyed from the central pool
even in powerful onshore winds.

PREVIOUS SPREAD, ABOVE AND OPPOSITE A wedge-shaped circulation with secret doors is created between different out-of-alignment wings. Horse riders from the local hunt often enjoy a refreshment in the motor court without dismounting. **FOLLOWING SPREAD** The house is in dialogue with the earth rampart archaeology of an ancient Māori *pā*, or fortified village, just discernible on the coastal razorback ridge in front.

HE TANGATA – IT IS PEOPLE

Once more:

What is the most important thing in the world?

He tangata, he tangata, he tangata.
It is people, it is people, it is people.

We are evolved beings. Our planet has shaped who we are, but now we are reshaping the planet, and in doing so we are reshaping ourselves and our descendants. More and more this is the imperative of our age.

In Western culture we often refer to a good building as 'having soul'. This involves a history, a 'living presence', where materials, scale and design are human or human-formed, allowing people to see themselves in the environment as a result. Architects

in every culture have known this for centuries; classicists know that if you create a building in the proportions of the human body people will consider it beautiful. But people also admire other human attributes, such as the honesty of brutalism, the clarity of modernism, the familiarity of the traditional.

However, today's questions are more about how will we build here? And what is the influence a building has on us and our sense of belonging and well-being? For New Zealanders this is called *wairuatanga*, the immutable connection between ourselves and our environment, whether natural or built.

In a growing body of literature on the relationship between the environment and people, writers and researchers have remarked on the significance of our experience of nature to our well-being, arguing that detachment from the health of the biosphere has meant a loss in our physical and emotional health. For us as architects, connection with nature involves a reciprocal relationship based on a world-view that sees humans as part of the environment and therefore our buildings and cities as part of this system too.

For us this means dialogue and commitment between key stakeholders, ecologists, builders, architects and creatives, communities, councils and *mana whenua* to ensure successful outcomes. In diverse discussions, long-term priorities prevail over a single focus. In New Zealand this is called *whanaungatanga*, or human relationships developed through the shared experience of working together. People are a key ingredient: it is often the clarity of the consciousness seen in an environment that gives us pleasure, a sense of care, belonging and well-being.

Leonardo da Vinci, *Vitruvian Man*, c.1490

WĀNAKA / 2021

Black Peak/Mount Burke is located on the shore of Lake Wānaka in New Zealand's South Island. It faces a group of five mountain peaks known as the Great Alpine Circle. The house is a retreat intended as an extension of our client family's formative years camping here in deep connection with the natural environment.

In a Māori creation myth, the land is considered as a mother figure, Papatūānuku, who married Ranginui, the sky father, forming the primordial couple from whom we are all believed to be descended. Mountains, rivers and other natural features all have identities within this tradition, and several of these have been granted legal personhood status under contemporary New Zealand law. Our clients' home is designed so their experience of the Alpine Circle is carefully choreographed into the home to form dialogue and connection to this outside 'family' of mountains.

Arrival in a sunny courtyard is greeted by axial views towards the first peak, Mount Burke, and an 'encampment' of buildings unfolds around this central, warm microclimate. The home's internal circulation is aligned with views of the second peak, Treble Cone, the location of the region's main ski resort. At the heart of the encampment are cooking and dining, with a series of layered views unfolding from the fireplace loggia towards the majestic summit of Black Peak, the highest in the Alpine Circle.

The home's extensive gardens are laid out for on-site food production, all energy is sustainably generated, water is harvested, and wastewater is ecologically reused. Reinforcing the building's sense of communion and belonging is a material palette carefully curated from the local environment. Stones sourced from the site itself form the base of the building and its fireplaces, while blackened larch cladding was charred by hand on-site, as were red cedar beams, columns and vertical fins.

PAGE 237 A mountain peak close to the house. **PREVIOUS SPREAD** A path leading up from the lake meanders lazily to the home's courtyard, while a stone skirt lowers the building's profile, connecting it to its mountain environment. A grove of poplar trees on the site was protected during construction and retained. **OPPOSITE** The home's charred larch entry is accessed via slabs of schist stone that were excavated and repurposed during construction. The entry leads into a sheltered courtyard containing a vegetable garden between a guest cottage and the main house.

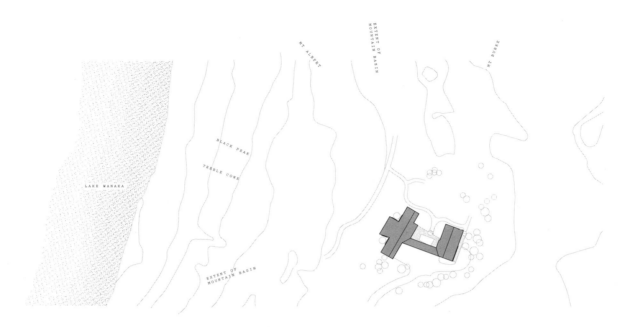

SITE PLAN

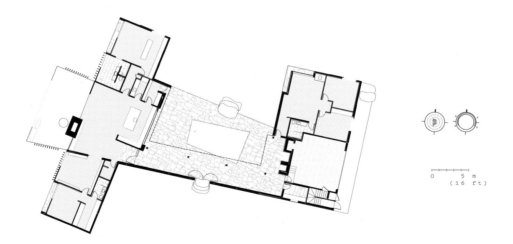

GROUND FLOOR PLAN

OPPOSITE The plan has been laid out to align with the surrounding mountain peaks, bringing them into a dialogue with everyday domestic life.

The interior of the house is furnished with French oak ceilings,
cabinetry and floors, charred larch walls and natural stone floors,
benches and vanities. The scents of these fill the house, mingling
with those of the lake.

ABOVE Outdoor dining is enjoyed among vegetable gardens and alongside the chef. **OPPOSITE** Views of the summit of Black Peak, the central mountain of the Alpine Circle, run along the home's main axis and terminate at the outdoor fireplace.

THREE FAMILY HOME

WAIHEKE / 2021

This family home is both monumental and minimalist. It is set in a secluded west-facing bay behind a golden sand beach. Its design responds to a familiar conundrum: families like to holiday together, but when children grow up and have their own children, then quite a crowd starts to form, all with disparate holiday wants. Often this is resolved over the generations with ad hoc additions set around an original home. But this family decided to build new.

The result is a multigenerational home, like a holiday resort where you have your own room or suite set around a mix of living and recreational spaces. You can ignore everyone and go for a nap, or you can take part in family activities, which often take place beside the swimming pool.

The organizing idea for the house is a cranked U shape, surrounding a large courtyard sheltered from both onshore and offshore winds. The landward arm of the U is set past the sea frontage to enable water views both around and through. The three wings are arranged for younger generations, older generations, and guests. They are quite porous, glazed both back and front to allow views through to the ocean and multiple circulation ways through the home. Every room has a connection to the outside via deep verandahs, and to a variety of extroverted and introverted spaces to enjoy according to sun, wind and mood.

Perhaps how a house operates is what gives an ease or almost a looseness to its sense of place. There is a formal entry into the home's seaward wing through large bronze doors, but day-to-day most people wander casually through its large central courtyard.

It is difficult to get a sense of both the scale and the intimacy from the photographs. For example, although the transoms above the doors are set at a lofty 3.2-metre (10½-foot) height, the bronze and marble details will become polished by hands and patinaed with time. Floors are a dark sustainable timber that will etch with sandy feet, matching walls of in-situ concrete, and timber board and batten cladding effortlessly flows from inside to out. The principal living areas share a monumental three-sided fireplace.

For us, the key to the design was in unifying concept and detail. Rather than being a conglomerate of smaller homes, the architecture is under one all-enveloping zigzag-shaped sculptural form. This abstracts nearby rows of the boatsheds for which the bay is named. The roof was achieved using a simple steel portal frame structure, with easy-to-build repeating details enabling what is quite a big house to be built simply and efficiently. We hope this home will feel as though it belongs on this beach and to this family for generations to come.

PREVIOUS SPREAD This bay is known for its weekend sailing regattas and for the rows of old gabled boatsheds that line the coast here. The sculptural silhouette of the house is designed to be in quiet affinity with all of this. **OPPOSITE** The house is laid out in a U shape, with three 'cranked' wings giving ocean views past and through. Oversized chain droppers function instead of downpipes.

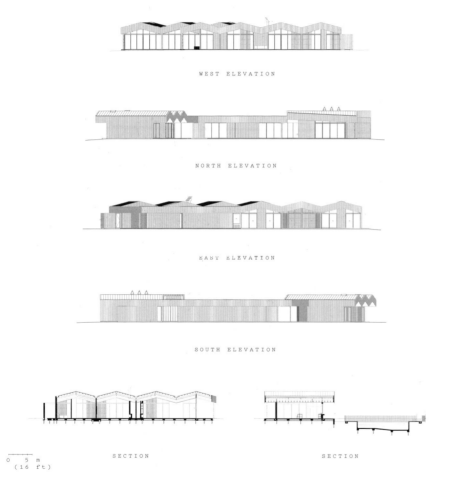

WEST ELEVATION

NORTH ELEVATION

EAST ELEVATION

SOUTH ELEVATION

SECTION

SECTION

0   5 m
(16 ft)

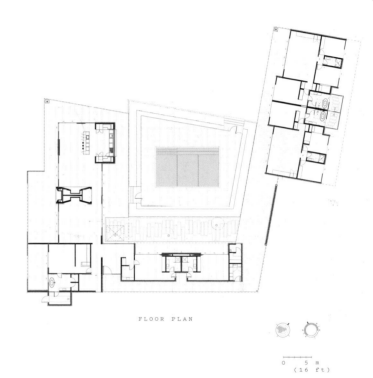

FLOOR PLAN

0   5 m
(16 ft)

OPPOSITE Parents, adult children and guests each have their own wing
around a central courtyard containing a sheltered sunken swimming pool.
The courtyard opens to forest on its fourth side.

253

OPPOSITE The home is unified with crisp, recessed detailing using a simple motif of vertical lines under a monumental sculptural roof. **ABOVE** Formal double-leaf bronze doors are accessed via a covered way, giving all-weather entry past the home's independent guest wing.

The seaward wing of the house contains a central concrete core made up of three matching fireplaces, one of which is exterior. The fireplace loggia facing the sea shelters under a sculptural zigzag roof.

TUCKER BEACH

Tucker Beach overlooks the Lower Shotover River in New Zealand's South Island. It is a short drive from popular holiday destinations, yet far enough away that it feels secluded and remote. Its owners had farmed on the site for many years before deciding to build.

Our aim was to ensure that the new home was deeply rooted in its landscape and connected to the owners' role as custodians of the land.

The house draws from the location's history as a working farm, taking cues from the agricultural relics of old barns and rusted machinery sheds dotted across the landscape. It is a collection of four simple shed forms set in a rugged environment, comprising guest cottage, winemaking, owners' accommodation and maintenance. All are clad in Corten steel set with raw concrete hearths: these untouched surfaces resonate with the surrounding bracken-clad landscape and its hues that change with the seasons - including those of a vineyard that forms part of the site.

The layout of the home is designed for authentic rural life. Arrival is via a farm track that threads together the four activities in sequence. Each building enjoys curated views of the meandering river below and the picturesque mountains above. Motorized awnings are easily opened and closed as the elements require. Areas in which to meet, socialize, dine and work are located in the spaces between the sheds, again with the focus on framing the surrounding landscape.

PREVIOUS SPREAD The home consists of four separate rural buildings clad in Corten steel, forming one sculptural composition in keeping with the natural landscape, especially when viewed from afar. A corner of the property's own vineyard can be glimpsed on the hillside above the house. **OPPOSITE** Rather than being set around a yard, sheds and farm buildings in New Zealand and Australia tend to collect incrementally along farm tracks. This gives buildings a meandering, informal lineal relationship to one another.

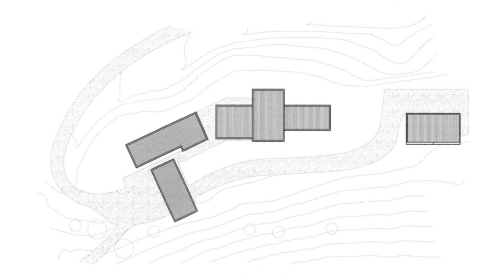

SITE PLAN

GROUND FLOOR PLAN

0   5 m
(16 ft)

OPPOSITE There is a focus on framing the surrounding landscape, with each building enjoying slightly different views out to the river and picturesque mountains beyond.

LEFT The kitchen sink: every domestic
activity here can be enjoyed with a view.
Robust awning shutters are operated
electronically. **OPPOSITE** A rugged farm
kitchen in blackened steel provides for
a welcoming and informal entry to the home.
FOLLOWING SPREAD Coming together outside
takes place in between the buildings,
where, again, the focus is on framing
the surrounding landscape. This terrace
is between the guest building and the
home's kitchen.

ANDREW PATTERSON, ARCHITECT

NZIA Gold Medal citation

Over the course of three decades Andrew Patterson has forged a reputation as a confident designer of striking buildings with great presence. His practice's portfolio is replete with distinctive projects. Patterson buildings do not just assert their difference against the designs of the architect's peers; they are also highly differentiated from each other. Consequently, Andrew's work epitomizes bespoke architecture and expresses the paradox of such particularity: he has generated a lineage uncharacterized by familial resemblance. He seems determined not to repeat himself.

That is not to say that Andrew's work is without defining traits or a common spirit. His architecture is as adventurous as he is aesthetically dexterous. He could surely turn his hand to any style, and like a high-art novelist dipping pseudonymously into genre writing, he has designed lesser-known works in a variety of idioms. But bold form-making is at the heart of Andrew's practice, along with an appreciation for and masterly deployment of materials. He likes the tough and solid stuff, especially concrete and steel.

This predilection is highly compatible with his declarative impulse. There is nothing tentative about Andrew's architecture. His is not a tread-lightly approach. Andrew's architecture is an architecture of occupation; buildings such as Site 3 (2001), Geyser (2012) and the Lodge at Kinloch Club (2016) take possession of their sites. Often, the buildings burrow in, as is the case with two Queenstown projects, AJ Hackett Bungy (2002) and the Michael Hill Golf Clubhouse (2008). Digging in, as Andrew points out, is not a foreign concept in this country; Māori were sculpting the earth in Aotearoa for centuries before the Europeans turned up.

Andrew is at least as comfortable talking about myths as about modernism. His attraction to mythologies, and the earth-moving and monument-making civilizations that have produced them, is expressed in strong formal statements such as Anvil and Local Rock House (both 2010) and the Len Lye Centre (2015). It also seems to feed his appetite for pattern-making, a hallmark of his architecture that is there for all to see on buildings as disparate as Cumulus (2003), Stratis (2005) and the Mai Mai house (2007). Pattern is not lightly applied to the façades of these buildings, but seemingly carved out of them. In Andrew's architecture clarity of concept is never betrayed by timidity of execution.

Unusually for a New Zealand architect, Andrew is not reticent about proclaiming his ambition and ability, or sharing his metaphorical excursions. The evocative nomenclature applied to many of his buildings – an amalgam of Platonic essentialism and capitalist branding – is a promise of excitement. As the late David Mitchell put it: 'Only an architect as courageous and skilled as Andrew can get away with fanning our expectations so flagrantly.' He gets away with it because his buildings consistently deliver on the promise of his concepts.

Andrew's potential was evident as a student – before he graduated he received the commission for his first house (at Karekare, completed in 1986) – and has been realized in a generation's worth of assured and often provocative buildings. The Summer Street House (1993), a Ponsonby 'urban bach' that substitutes steel wall for picket fence, was an early, and in this case literal, manifestation of his willingness to push the boundaries. Andrew's professional progress has been paved with architecture awards. All along, he has demonstrated an enviable facility for making the most of a project's design possibilities, and has long demonstrated a capacity to take a client along with him on an intrepid journey. He has a keen eye for talent; several of his senior staff have become significant practitioners in their own right. He has also gone where few New Zealand architects venture, into the big, wide world, designing, for example, the New Zealand Pavilion at the 2012 Frankfurt Book Fair and the New Zealand China Concept Store in Shanghai (2014).

Well into the middle part of his career, Andrew keeps growing, and his buildings keep surprising. Latterly, and significantly in post-earthquake Canterbury, his practice has applied a sensitive touch to the Christchurch Botanic Gardens Visitor Centre (2013) and dwellings (2013-2016) at Annandale on Banks Peninsula. Andrew is a singular figure in this country's architecture, a star following his own orbit. He is a most worthy winner of the New Zealand Institute of Architects Gold Medal.

The New Zealand Institute of Architects

PATTERSON ASSOCIATES

Andrew Patterson founded his eponymous architecture practice in 1986 and now leads it with his fellow directors Andrew Mitchell and Davor Popadich. Patterson designs for clients and sites globally but continues to be based in its studio, Luminous, in the heart of New Zealand's architecture district in Parnell, Auckland. Its work spans civic, commercial, exhibition and urban design, and of course residential.

Pattersons.com

DAVOR POPADICH
(Photography: Northland Farmhouse)

Ranging across the disciplines of architecture, photography, and digital film and image, Davor Popadich's work engages with perceptions of space, nature, terrain and locality. Davor holds a Bachelor of Architecture degree with 1st class honours from the University of Auckland School of Architecture, and in 2013 he was admitted as a Fellow of the New Zealand Institute of Architects. Davor is a director at Patterson Associates and an inaugural member of the Board of Studies at the University of Auckland, School of Architecture. He lives and works in Auckland.

SIMON DEVITT
(Photography, unless otherwise stated)

Simon Devitt is an Auckland-based photographer with a practice focus on architecture. His work is published in numerous national and international magazines, including *Elle Decor Italia*, *Architectural Digest* (Germany), *Dwell* (USA), *Habitus*, *InDesign* (Australia), *Architecture NZ*, *Urbis*, *Interior* (NZ).

Simon's images also feature in many books, including Julia Gatley's Auckland University Press-published *Long Live the Modern* (2009), *Group Architects: Towards a New Zealand Architecture* (2010) and *Athfield Architects* (2012). In 2013 Devitt launched his first self-published photo-book, *Portrait of a House*, on the Athfield residence in Wellington. He followed this in 2016 with *Rannoch*, about the life and home of New Zealand arts patron Sir James Wallace. *Rannoch* has gone on to win New Zealand photo-book of the year and won at the German Design Council Awards in 2018. Simon lectures in Photography of Architecture at the University of Auckland.

JENNY ANDERSON
(Interior Design: Seascape, Local Rock House and Waiheke)

Jenny Anderson trained and practised in interior design initially in London before returning to New Zealand in the late 1980s. Her passion is for texture and colour. Jenny's refined sense of luxury results in the creation of beautiful bespoke spaces that are tailored to each client. Jenny has collaborated with Patterson Associates on many projects, including Seascape, Local Rock House and Waiheke houses.

GLOSSARY OF MĀORI TERMS

Aotearoa
The Māori name for New Zealand. It is loosely translated as 'the land of the long white cloud'.

kaitiakitanga
Guardianship. Traditionally, Māori believe there is a deep kinship between humans and the natural world. This connection is expressed through *kaitiakitanga*.

mana whenua
The original people of the land.

marae
Courtyard of the tribal meeting house.

Ranginui and Papatūānuku
The Sky Father and the Earth Mother.

Te Ika-a-Māui
New Zealand's North Island.

Te Waipounamu
New Zealand's South Island.

wairuatanga
The connection between us and our environment.

whakapapa
Genealogy. *Whakapapa* links people to all other living things and to the earth and sky, and it traces the universe back to its origins.

whanaungatanga
Human relationships developed through the shared experience of working together.

wharenui
Meeting house, or main building of the *marae* where guests are greeted and accommodated.

ACKNOWLEDGMENTS

My sincere thanks to our clients, and particularly those who have generously allowed us to include their homes in this book.

Thank you to the consultants and contractors who we are lucky enough to work with to bring these projects to life.

Thank you to Tere Insley for reviewing the Māori content.

And a special thank you to my team at Patterson Associates. Thanks to my CEO Kerry Marshall, my directors and associates Andrew Mitchell, Davor Popadich, Surya Fullerton, Shane Taylor, Luke Douglas, Sajeev Ruthramoorthy and Richard Andrews. As well as to the team that worked on this book: Emma Haughton, Nicole Allan, George Grieve, David Moore, Patrick Sherwood, Cindy Huang, Sam Moloney and Michaella Franklin.

On the front cover: Scrubby Bay (see page 40)
On the back cover: Seascape Retreat (see page 26)
Page 1: Andrew Patterson's first conceptual sketch for Mai Mai, 2006
Pages 4-5: Seascape Retreat
Pages 6-7: Bethells Beach, view from the house
Pages 8-9: The Michael Hill Clubhouse

First published in the United Kingdom in 2018
by Thames & Hudson Ltd, 181A High Holborn, London WC1V 7QX

This revised and updated edition published in 2023

Patterson: Houses of Aotearoa © 2018 and 2023 Thames & Hudson Ltd, London
Text and plans © 2018 and 2023 Patterson Associates
Foreword © 2018 Herbert Ypma
For all other illustrations, please see the
picture credits list on page 271.

Designed by Steve Russell / aka-designaholic.com

British Library Cataloguing-in-Publication Data
A catalogue record for this book is available from the British Library

ISBN 978-0-500-02645-8

Printed in China by Shanghai Offset Printing Products Limited

Be the first to know about our new releases,
exclusive content and author events by visiting
thamesandhudson.com
thamesandhudsonusa.com
thamesandhudson.com.au